MY SUBURBAN COMMUNITY

Portia Summers

Enslow Publishing
101 W. 23rd Street
Suite 240
New York, NY 10011
USA

enslow.com

WORDS TO KNOW

community—A group of people who live and work together.

goods—Things that people can buy and sell.

mobile—Moveable.

pediatrician—A doctor who treats children.

postal—Having to do with the mail.

public—All the people in a town, city, state, or country, or something that all the people own together and share.

services—Things that people do for other people.

suburb—A town that is outside the limits of a city but not far out in the country.

volunteers—People who do work without being paid.

CONTENTS

A suburban community is great for people who want a quiet neighborhood that is not too far from a city.

What Is a Suburban Community?

A group of people who live and work together are called a
community. A suburban community is a place that is near a
city. Many people who live in the suburbs drive or take a train
to the city for work. People have more space in the suburbs
than people do in a city. Neighbors live closer together in the
suburbs than in the country.

Growing Up in a Suburban Community

Children in the suburbs live in all different kinds of homes. Some live in houses. Some live in small apartment buildings. Some live in mobile homes. They all go to school together. They have friends from different places around the community.

School Events

People from the community go to all kinds of events at the school. Even grown-ups without children in the school go to the events. They come to see band concerts and school plays. They come to see football games and art shows.

Community members gather together for a high school football game.

People Who Help

There are many people who help others in a suburban community. Doctors, police officers, and firefighters all work hard to make sure that the people in the community stay healthy and safe.

Doctors

A pediatrician is a doctor who takes care of children. The pediatrician has an office in the community. She also works with the local hospital. Children who become very sick can get special care there.

A pediatrician is an important member of the community.

Police Officers

Police officers protect the community. They drive around the community in their police cars. They also get around on bicycles and on foot.

Police officers make sure that everyone follows the community's rules. They put people who hurt other people or who take other people's things in jail. They make sure that people drive safely on the roads.

Firefighters

In some big communities being a firefighter is a full-time job. In many suburban communities, firefighters are volunteers. They have other jobs that they do to earn money. When there is a fire, they stop whatever they are doing. They hurry to the fire station.

Firefighters work together to fight fires. They keep the people, homes, and businesses in their community safe.

Places to Go

There are many places to go and things to do in the suburbs. It is usually just a short car ride to shops, restaurants, the library, or a park. People of all ages have places where they can gather to see friends who enjoy the same things that they do.

The YMCA

The YMCA is a suburban community center. The YMCA has a swimming pool, a place to play sports, and classrooms.

Children and adults can learn to swim and to play different sports.

People can take classes at the YMCA. They can get together with a group for a meeting. The YMCA is a place in the community where everyone can get together.

Playing basketball is one way community members can have fun at the YMCA.

Going Out to Eat

Business owners are a part of the suburban community, too. The owner of the coffee shop serves food and drinks to many people in the town. People come together at the coffee shop. They meet to share news each week.

People in the community work at the shop. The waitress lives in town. She walks to work each day. Local teenagers wash dishes in the kitchen.

Important Business

Business owners sell things that people in their communities want and need. They also give people jobs, so that they can earn money to buy things that they want and need.

In a suburban community, people often get together at restaurants or coffee shops.

Serving the Community

People in a suburban community need help keeping the area clean and safe. Homes may need to be fixed, roads may need to cleared, and mail needs to be delivered. These are all services that people in the suburbs need. Often the town will take care of these services.

Town Workers

Town workers clean the roads when it snows. They make sure that water pipes bring fresh water to people's homes. People need the water to drink and to cook. The public pays taxes so that the town workers have everything they need to do their jobs.

A town worker helps to fix a road.

Delivering the Mail

Postal workers are an important part of the suburban community. Everyone loves to get a letter or a birthday card in the mail. Important letters and bills also come in the mail. The people at the post office work to make sure that people in the community receive their mail.

Some postal workers sort mail. Others sell stamps at the counter. Letter carriers carry the mail to homes and businesses in the community.

How Did That Get Here?

Your mail carrier might deliver your mail to your home on foot or in a truck. But before that, your letter or package might travel on a plane, train, or boat before it gets to you!

A mail carrier in a suburban community will sometimes walk from house to house to deliver the mail.

Working Together in the Suburbs

People in a suburban community help each other. They buy and sell the goods and services they want and need. They work for businesses and for the government. They volunteer at the fire department. They help their neighbors when they have problems. They celebrate together when they are happy.

As part of a suburban community, people like to spend time having fun and getting to know each other.

ACTIVITY: COMPARING COMMUNITIES

A suburban community is different from a city (urban) community or a country (rural) community. For example, a city has more people than the country. A suburb has fewer houses than a city. Let's compare a suburban community with the city or the country. How are they the same? How are they different?

1. Copy down the diagram on p. 23. Label one circle "Suburban" and the other circle "Urban" or "Rural."

2. In the middle of the diagram, list some people who you would find in both communities, like a police officer or a doctor.

3. At the outer parts of the circles, list people who you would probably find in only one of the communities (such as a farmer in a rural community and a taxi driver in an urban community).

4. Now think of the places you would find in the two communities. What kind of places would you find in both? What kind of places would only be in one community?

5. Can you think of other ways to compare the two communities? Some ideas to think about: How do kids get to school? What activities do people do for fun?

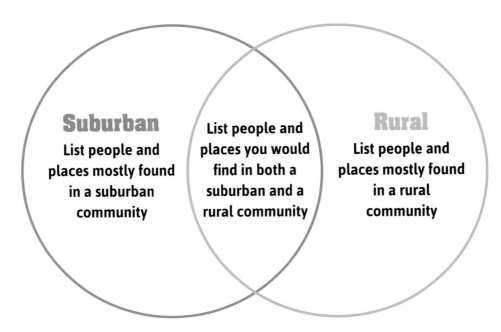

Suburban
List people and places mostly found in a suburban community

List people and places you would find in both a suburban and a rural community

Rural
List people and places mostly found in a rural community

LEARN MORE

Books

Austen, Mary. *We Live in a Suburb.* New York: PowerKids Press, 2016.

Kreisman, Rachelle. *People Who Help: A Kids' Guide to Community Helpers.* South Egremont, MA: Red Chair Press, 2015.

Rhatigan, Joe. *People You Gotta Meet Before You Grow Up: Get to Know the Movers and Shakers in Your Hometown.* Watertown, MA: Charlesbridge, 2014.

Waldron, Melanie. *Mapping Communities.* Chicago: Raintree, 2013.

Websites

Education Place
www.eduplace.com/kids/socsci/books/applications/imaps/maps/g3_u1/index.html
Explore an interactive map of three types of communities.

American Planning Association
www.planning.org/kidsandcommunity/
Do fun activities and learn more about communit

INDEX

Published in 2017 by Enslow Publishing, LLC.
101 W. 23rd Street, Suite 240, New York, NY 10011
Copyright © 2017 by Enslow Publishing, LLC

All rights reserved.

No part of this book may be reproduced by any means without the written permission of the publisher.

Library of Congress Cataloging-in-Publication Data
Names: Summers, Portia.
Title: My suburban community / Portia Summers.
Description: New York : Enslow Publishing, 2017 | Series: Zoom in on communities | Audience: K to Grade 3. | Includes bibliographical references and index.
Identifiers: ISBN 978-0-7660-7835-2 (library bound) | ISBN 978-0-7660-7833-8 (pbk.) | ISBN 978-0-7660-7834-5 (6 pack)
Subjects: LCSH: Suburban life--Juvenile literature. | Suburbs--Juvenile literature. | Communities--Juvenile literature.
Classification: LCC HT351.S96 2017 | DDC 307.74--dc23

Printed in Malaysia

To Our Readers: We have done our best to make sure all website addresses in this book were active and appropriate when we went to press. However, the author and the publisher have no control over and assume no liability for the material available on those websites or on any websites they may link to. Any comments or suggestions can be sent by e-mail to customerservice@enslow.com.

Photo Credits: Cover, p. 1 rSnapshotPhotos/Shutterstock.com; graphics throughout Kev Draws/Shutterstock.com (people circle), antoshkaforever/Shutterstock.com (people holding hands), 3d_kot/Shutterstock.com (houses); p. 4 iStock.com/brennanwesley; p. 7 Ron Jenkins/Fort Worth Star-Telegram/MCT via Getty Images; p. 9 Pressmaster/Shutterstock.com; p. 10 Upper Cut Images/Getty Images; p. 11 iStock.com/Valerie Loiseleux; p. 13 Glenn Asakawa/The Denver Post via Getty Images; p. 15 Monkeybusinessimages/iStock/Thinkstock; p. 17 Kadmy/iStock/Thinkstock; p. 19 Andrew Harrer/Bloomberg via Getty Images; p. 21 Hero Images Inc./SuperStock.